920
BSI zno. 1

Issue #1
Spring 2007

biography
for
beginners

Sketches for Early Readers

Laurie Lanzen Harris,
Editor

Favorable Impressions

P.O. Box 69018
Pleasant Ridge, Michigan 48069

Laurie Lanzen Harris, *Editor and Publisher*
Dan Harris, *Vice President, Marketing*
Frank Abate, *Sketch Writer*
Favorable Impressions
P.O. Box 69018, Pleasant Ridge, Michigan 48069

ISSN 1081-4973

The information in this publication was compiled from the sources cited and from other sources considered reliable. While every possible effort has been made to ensure reliability, the publisher will not assume liability for damages caused by inaccuracies in the data, and makes no warranty, express or implied, on the accuracy of the information contained herein.

(∞)

This book is printed on acid-free paper meeting the ANSI Z39.48 Standard. The infinity symbol that appears above indicates that the paper in this book meets that standard.

Printed in the United States

Contents

Preface

Biography for Beginners is a publication designed for young readers ages 6 to 9. It covers the kinds of people young people want to know about—favorite authors, television and sports stars, and world figures.

Biography for Beginners is published two times a year. A one-year subscription includes two 100-page hardbound volumes, published in Spring (May) and Fall (October).

The Plan of the Work

Biography for Beginners is especially created for young readers in a format they can read, understand, and enjoy. Each hardcover issue contains approximately 10 profiles, arranged alphabetically. Each entry provides several illustrations, including photographs of the individual, book covers, illustrations from books, and action shots. Each entry is coded with a symbol that indicates the profession of the person profiled. Boldfaced headings lead readers to information on birth, growing up, school, choosing a career, work life, and home and family. Each entry concludes with an address so that students can write for further information. Web sites are included as available. The length and vocabulary used in each entry, as well as the type size, page size, illustrations, and layout, have been developed with early readers in mind.

Because an early reader's first introduction to biography often comes as part of a unit on a writer like Dr. Seuss, authors are a special focus of *Biography for Beginners*. The authors included in this issue were chosen for their appeal to readers in grades one through four.

There is a broad range of reading abilities in children ages 6 to 9. A book that would appeal to a beginning first-grade reader might not satisfy the needs of an advanced reader finishing the fourth grade. To accommodate the widest range of readers in the age group, *Biography for Beginners* is written at the mid-second grade to third grade reading level. If beginning readers find the content too difficult, the entry could be used as a "read aloud" text, or readers could use the boldfaced headings to focus on parts of a sketch.

Indexes

Each issue of *Biography for Beginners* includes a Name Index, a Subject Index covering occupations and ethnic and minority backgrounds, and a Birthday Index. These indexes cumulate with each issue. The indexes are intended to be used by the young readers themselves, with help from teachers and librarians, and are not as detailed or lengthy as the indexes in works for older children.

Our Advisors

Biography for Beginners was reviewed by an Advisory Board made up of school librarians, public librarians, and reading specialists. Their thoughtful comments and suggestions have been invaluable in developing this publication. Any errors, however, are mine alone. I would like to list the members of the Advisory Board and to thank them again for their efforts.

Linda Carpino   Detroit Public Library
Detroit, MI

Nina Levine   Blue Mountain Middle School
Cortlandt Manor, NY

Nancy Margolin   McDougle Elementary School
Chapel Hill, NC

Deb Rothaug   Plainview Old Bethpage Schools
Plainview, NY

Laurie Scott   Farmington Hills Community Library
Farmington Hills, MI

Joyce Siler   Westridge Elementary School
Kansas City, MO

Your Comments Are Welcome

Our goal is to provide accurate, accessible biographical information to early readers. Let us know how you think we're doing. Please write or call me with your comments.

We want to include the people your young readers want to know about. Send me your suggestions to the address below, or to my e-mail address. You can also post suggestions at our website, www.favimp.com. If we include someone you or a young reader suggest, we will send you a free issue, with our compliments, and we'll list your name in the issue in which your suggested profile appears.

And take a look at the next page, where we've listed those libraries and individuals who will be receiving a free copy of this issue for their suggestions.

Acknowledgments

I'd like to thank Mary Ann Stavros for superb design, layout, and typesetting; Catherine Harris for editorial assistance; Barry Puckett for research assistance; and Kevin Hayes for production help.

Laurie Harris
Editor, *Biography for Beginners*
P.O. Box 69018
Pleasant Ridge, MI 48069
e-mail: laurieh@favimp.com
URL: http://www.favimp.com

CONGRATULATIONS!

Congratulations to the following individuals and libraries, who are receiving a free copy of *Biography for Beginners*, Spring 2007, for suggesting people who appear in this issue:

Sister Jeanette Adler, Pine Ridge Elementary, Birdseye, IN

Carol Blaney, Conley Elementary, Whitman, MA

Karen Locke, McKean Elementary, McKean, PA

Nancy Margolin, McDougle Elementary, Chapel Hill, NC

Deb Rothaug, Pasadena Elementary, Plainview, NY

Jean de Brunhoff
1899-1937
French Children's Author and Illustrator
Creator of *Babar*

JEAN DE BRUNHOFF WAS BORN on December 9, 1899, in Paris, France. His parents were Maurice and Marguerite de Brunhoff. (His last name is pronounced "BREW-noff.") Maurice was a magazine publisher and Marguerite was a homemaker. Jean was the youngest of four children.

JEAN DE BRUNHOFF GREW UP in Paris, loving art and drawing.

JEAN DE BRUNHOFF WENT TO SCHOOL in Paris. After high school, he studied art at the L'Ecole Alsacienne. His studies were interrupted by World War I (1914-1918). When the war was over, he returned to Paris to study art.

STARTING TO WORK AS AN ARTIST: By the 1920s, Brunhoff was making his living as an artist. He displayed his paintings in galleries, and was also a successful portrait painter.

CREATING BABAR: In 1924, Brunhoff married Cecile Sabouraud, a musician. Soon, they had two sons, Laurent and Mathieu. Cecile created the character we all know and love as Babar as a bedtime story for the boys. (She called him "little elephant.")

The boys loved the tale of the little elephant. They told their father about him, and Brunhoff was inspired to draw him, and to give him a name. Those first drawings developed into the first book, *The Story of Babar: The Little Elephant.*

Brunhoff's family and friends were delighted with the story and paintings. They encouraged him to publish the book. One of his brothers was a publisher,

so, in 1931, *The Story of Babar* appeared in France. It immediately became a favorite. Soon, it was published

in English, then in many other languages. A classic children's character had been born.

THE STORY OF BABAR, THE LITTLE ELEPHANT: As millions of readers know, Babar is an elephant who grows from youth to adulthood in the books. His story starts out sadly: his mother is shot by a wicked hunter. Alone, Babar makes his way to the world of people. A kind old lady takes him in, gives him money, and teaches him the ways of humans. Soon, Babar is a finely dressed, curious, and distinguished member of society.

Brunhoff wrote six more Babar books, each a great success. In *The Travels of Babar*, readers are introduced to more delightful new characters. These include Celeste, who becomes Babar's wife and his queen.

Babar the King features Babar's adventures in the animal world as King. These books also feature the delightful old Cornelius, advisor to Babar. In *Babar and His Children*, Babar and Celeste become the parents of triplets. So the adventures of Pom, Flora, and Alexander become part of the tales. Their mischief-making cousin, Arthur, joins in the fun.

Each of the books is beautifully illustrated, with large, two-page spreads full of detail. Children enjoy looking at the pages over and over. They discover something new each time. The tone of the books is warm and witty. They charm readers — and listeners — of all ages.

Sadly, in the 1930s, Brunhoff learned he had tuberculosis. The disease destroys the lungs. When Brunhoff was diagnosed, there was no cure. He had to move to a sanatorium, away from his family. From there, he continued to send the stories of Babar to his children, often as part of his letters.

BABAR AND FATHER CHRISTMAS: Jean de Brunhoff's final book was *Babar and Father Christmas*. This delightful tale tells how Babar helps Father Christmas back to health. To thank him, Father Christmas helps Babar's family celebrate Christmas in a special way.

LAURENT DE BRUNHOFF AND THE CONTINUATION OF BABAR: Tragically, Jean de Brunhoff died of tuberculosis on October 16, 1937. He was 37 years old. His son Laurent was only 12 when his father died. Like his father, Laurent was a talented artist. When he was 21, he decided to continue his father's work. In 1946, he began to write and illustrate books about Babar.

The style and wit of Laurent's books are so much like his father's that many people never noticed a different Brunhoff had created them. In the past 60 years, Laurent has published more than 30 new Babar books. These beloved books have been translated into 17 languages and sold millions of copies. They keep alive a timeless character who has captured the imaginations of children for more than 70 years.

JEAN DE BRUNHOFF'S HOME AND FAMILY: Brunhoff married his wife Cecile in 1924. They had three sons,

Laurent, Mathieu, and Thierry. It was Cecile who first created the character of Babar, for her young sons.

JEAN DE BRUNHOFF'S BOOKS:

The Story of Babar, the Little Elephant
The Travels of Babar
Babar the King
ABC of Babar
Babar and Zephir
Babar and His Children
Babar and Father Christmas

FOR MORE INFORMATION ABOUT JEAN DE BRUN-HOFF:

Write: Random House
Publicity Dept.
1745 Broadway
New York, NY 10019

WORLD WIDE WEB SITES:

http://prose.web.wesleyan.edu/Babar/family.htm
http://www.themorgan.org/about/pressReleases2.asp

Kevin Clash
1960-
American Puppeteer for *Sesame Street*
Creator of Elmo

KEVIN CLASH WAS BORN on September 17, 1960, in Baltimore, Maryland. His family lived in Turner's Station, Maryland, and a suburb of Baltimore. His parents are Gladys and George Clash. Gladys ran a daycare center in the family home. George was a welder. Kevin is one of four kids. He has one brother, George Jr., and two sisters, Anita and Pam.

KEVIN CLASH GREW UP a shy but creative child. "I loved to draw and build things," he recalls. His parents, who've always supported his talent, encouraged him. He also remembers loving children television shows like *Sesame Street* and *Captain Kangaroo*. He sat inches away from the set, studying and drawing puppets, to understand how they were built. "My goal was to figure out how they made the Muppets so you couldn't see any seams," he recalls. He also became a "serious people-watcher."

Kevin's first puppeteering was for the kids in his Mom's daycare. Using a "blanket strung over the clothesline for a makeshift stage," he delighted that first audience. Soon, Kevin learned to sew and was making his own puppets. He used whatever he could find: "old buttons, fabric, a worn-out fuzzy slipper, odd bits of plastic or Styrofoam."

Sometimes, his hobby led to teasing. "Look at him," neighbor kids would say. "He's playing with dolls. He sews. He sleeps with his puppets." His parents' friends told them Kevin should be outside playing sports. But his parents supported him. "Because they had the strength to ignore all of that, so could I," he recalls.

KEVIN CLASH WENT TO SCHOOL at the local public schools. His talent led him to creative ways to complete assignments. In middle school, he created a puppet show instead of writing a paper for a history assignment. The teacher gave him an "A." Later, he put on the show for all the students.

Soon, Clash was doing live puppet shows in and around the Baltimore area. By the time he was 15, local personality Stu Kerr spotted him at one of his shows and asked Clash to work on his local TV show, "Caboose," as a puppeteer. He was really getting noticed.

Some one else who noticed was Kermit Love, who designed Muppets for Jim Henson. He was invited to help out on the Sesame Street float at the Thanksgiving Parade in New York City. He was only 17. It was an amazing experience. He knew that he wanted to become a professional puppeteer.

STARTING TO WORK WITH JIM HENSON: In 1985, Clash started working regularly with Jim Henson. He worked with the Muppets on *Sesame Street* and other productions, too. It was a dream come true. Clash says his life feels like a fairy tale sometimes. This was just the beginning.

EARLY MUPPETS: Clash's early work with Henson included TV and movies. He worked on the TV shows *Jim Henson Hour* and *Muppets Tonight.* His movie work included *The Labyrinth*, *Muppet Treasure Island,* and *Teenage Mutant Ninja Turtles* I and II.

The Sesame Street Muppets

One of Clash's earliest *Sesame Street* assignments was Hoots the Owl. This wise old bird is a jazz musician. Clash was so delighted to be a Muppetteer he loved doing any character. He remembers playing "chickens and pigs and AMs (Anything Muppets), clucking and oinking (and barking, squeaking, or hooting)." But it was his creation of a loveable, furry red monster that made him famous.

THE CREATION OF ELMO: One day in 1983, Master Henson Muppeteer Richard Hunt tossed Clash a "shapeless, soft bundle of red that I caught in midair."

Hunt yelled, "give it a voice!" "I grabbed the little monster and put him high on my arm," he recalls. Then, the puppet "let loose with a boundless, childlike laugh — a falsetto squeal that would change my life."

"'Hello, it's Elmo'! called this creature in the happiest of voices. 'Hi, everybody!'" A star was born. For the past 22 years, Clash has made Elmo come to life for millions of kids around the world.

Since Elmo's first appearance, as a "young monster," he's grown to be a favorite character on *Sesame Street*. He was created in part to appeal to the show's younger audience. Clash performs him as a 3½ year old. Kids see the world through Elmo's eyes as he lives and learns on Sesame Street.

Paula Abdul with Zoe and Elmo

TICKLE ME ELMO: In 1996, a toy plush Elmo doll took the market by storm. Before Christmas of that year 5 million "Tickle Me Elmo" dolls, with the character's signature laugh, were sold to happy kids everywhere.

Clash was amazed and surprised to hear that laugh wherever he went.

KIDS AND ELMO: Clash is astonished at Elmo's affect on kids. "When I'm doing a live appearance with Elmo, the kids don't really see me. They are focused on their friend they see on TV. I'm amazed at what happens when I have him look directly into their eyes, put his arms around them for a hug and a kiss. As Elmo comes to life with these displays of affection, so do the children."

For many fans, finding out that Elmo is the creation of a black man is a surprise. "I do like when African-Americans see me and see that I'm black," he says. He's now the senior puppet coordinator for all the Muppets on *Sesame Street.*

Clash is also co-executive producer of "Elmo's World." This is a special part of the TV show about Elmo and his friends. Mo Willems, who appears in this issue of *Biography for Beginners,* helped create " Elmo's World. " Clash's job is demanding, and he often works 16-hour days. It's physically hard, too. He has to scrunch his 6-foot body behind a screen. Then he projects all the feeling he can into the voice of a puppet. It's acting, but he can't use his own face and body to get his thoughts across. He also is involved in the script process and rehearsing the many scenes that go into a day's production.

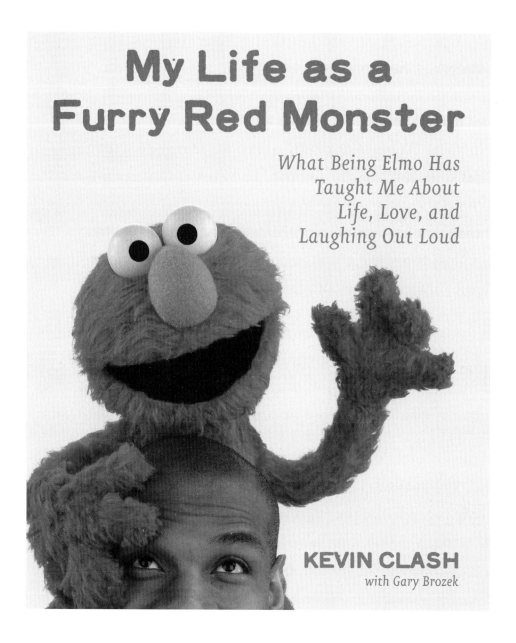

My Life as a
Furry Red Monster

*What Being Elmo Has
Taught Me About
Life, Love, and
Laughing Out Loud*

KEVIN CLASH

with *Gary Brozek*

Clash loves his work, and loving fans and fame in the world of television have rewarded him. He's won nine Emmy Awards. Three are for Outstanding Performer in a Children Series, and six are for Co-Producer of a Preschool Children's Series.

Despite the work and fame, Clash always finds time for kids. He visits them in hospitals and schools all over the world with Elmo. These two ambassadors of laughter and love are welcome wherever they go.

KEVIN CLASH'S HOME AND FAMILY: Kevin Clash is now divorced from his wife, Genia. They have one daughter, Shannon. They are still a very close family and still spend time together. Like her dad, Shannon loves art.

QUOTE

"When I am performing Elmo in front of a camera, I remind myself that somewhere out there, there's a kid perched as close to the television as I used to sit, wanting to reach through the screen to touch and be touched. Like Elmo, I strive to touch the heart of every child I come into contact with."

SOME OF KEVIN CLASH'S CREDITS:

Television

Captain Kangaroo: 1979
The Great Space Caper: 1979
Sesame Street: 1985–

Jim Henson Hour
Muppets Tonight!
Dinosaurs
Elmopalooza
Elmo Saves Christmas
Cinderelmo

Movies

Labyrinth
Muppet Treasure Island
Teenage Mutant Ninja Turtles I and *II*
Elmo in Grouchland
Muppets in Space

FOR MORE INFORMATION ABOUT KEVIN CLASH:

Write: Random House
      Broadway Books
      1745 Broadway
      New York, NY 10019

WORLD WIDE WEB SITES:

http://www.cnn.com/SPECIALS/2002/black.history/stories/28.clash/ http://www.kevinclashbook.com http://www.randomhouse.com/broadway/furryred monster/kevin_clash/

Katie Couric

1957-
American Television Journalist
Anchor of *CBS Evening News*
with Katie Couric
First Woman to be Solo Anchor for an
Evening Network News Show

KATIE COURIC WAS BORN on January 7, 1957, in Arlington, Virginia. Her full name is Katherine Anne

Couric. Her parents are John and Elinor Couric. John is a retired journalist and Elinor is a homemaker. Katie was the youngest of four children. She had two sisters, Emily and Clara, and a brother, John.

KATIE COURIC GREW UP in a large, happy family. She was outgoing and athletic, and always had lots of friends.

KATIE COURIC WENT TO SCHOOL at the local public schools. She was an excellent student and an athlete, too. At Yorktown High School, she worked on the school newspaper and was a member of the National Honor Society. She competed in track and gymnastics, and was a cheerleader, too.

After graduating from high school, Couric went to college at the University of Virginia. She earned her degree in English and American Studies in 1979.

FIRST JOBS: Couric moved to Washington, D.C., and started her career in journalism. She got a job with ABC as an assistant. She worked with some of the biggest names in TV news. But the work was boring. She spent a lot of time getting coffee and sandwiches for the newsmen. She needed more of a challenge.

Couric's next job was with CNN. She worked there for four years, traveling the country as a producer and reporter. Next, she worked for WTVJ in Miami for two years. Still wanting to learn more, she took a job with WRC-TV in Washington. That station was owned by NBC, and it was the beginning of a 20-year career with the network.

The job at WRC involved covering all kinds of stories—crime, politics, and features, too. After a few years, she moved on to NBC network news. Now, she had a national beat, covering the Pentagon. (That's the home of the U.S. military in Washington.) Couric was noticed by NBC's Tim Russert, who admired her work. "She was always so competent and unflustered," he said.

Soon, Couric was covering major national news stories. In 1990, she anchored the weekend news for NBC. Next, she was selected to work on one of NBC's top shows, *Today.*

THE TODAY SHOW: Couric joined the *Today* show as a national correspondent. In that job, she covered international news. She traveled the world, reporting on elections and world events. Couric became known as an engaging and accurate reporter.

In 1991, she began filling in as co-host of *Today*, with Bryant Gumbel. She was such a hit with viewers that she was offered the job of co-host full-time. She stayed

*Couric and Co-Host Matt Lauer from the Set
of the Today Show*

with the show for 15 years. She helped make it the top-rated morning show in the country.

Over those 15 years, Couric was known for her charm and warmth, but she could be a tough newsperson, too. She interviewed every President and major political figure, and entertainment stars, too. She covered breaking news stories, and was often the first to get important interviews.

In 1993, she added another NBC news show to her workload, *Now, with Tom Brokaw and Katie Couric.* That made for a very busy schedule, but she loved it. In 1997, Bryant Gumbel retired, and Couric got a new co-host, Matt Lauer.

The job was demanding, and Couric worked hard. She left home at 4:30 in the morning, and regularly worked 14 hours a day. But she loved her job.

A FAMILY TRAGEDY: In 1998, Couric's husband, Jay Monahan, died of colon cancer. It was a terrible shock. Couric took a month off from the show. When she returned, she had a new mission. She became an outspoken advocate for early screening for cancer. She was tireless in her efforts to reach out to Americans.

Couric took this message to the world: with early screening and treatment, colon cancer is beatable. Within several years, surveys showed that colon cancer deaths were down 20%. Some called those results the "Couric effect." Her TV reports on cancer won her praise and awards. She received a Peabody Award in 2000. That's one of the highest honors in broadcasting. Couric also won six Emmys for her work on *Today*.

Couric was one of the most popular figures on television. Viewers loved her warm, down-to-earth style. She could move from a serious news story to an interview with a pop star, and always seem prepared and engaging. She also became the highest paid person on television, making $14 million a year. And she even found time to write children's books.

THE CBS EVENING NEWS WITH KATIE COURIC: In 2006, Couric made the decision to leave the *Today* show to take on an even bigger role. She became the anchor for the *CBS Evening News*. She is the first woman to anchor an evening network news show alone. It was a tough decision to make. She'd been with *Today* for 15 years, and she was a star. Taking on a new assignment, she had no idea if she'd succeed. "Every time you make a big change that gets a lot of attention it's a bit anxiety-producing. I just hope this is fun. I said to the people at CBS, 'This better be fun'."

Couric took over her new job on September 5, 2006. At first, her ratings soared. But after a few months, the broadcast fell to third place, behind the ABC and NBC evening newscasts. Couric remains upbeat. She anchored CBS's coverage of the national election in 2006, and impressed many people.

She's also the managing editor of the newscast. That means that she decides what stories will be covered. She's also contributing to CBS's hit show *60 Minutes* and heading up TV specials, too.

KATIE COURIC'S HOME AND FAMILY: Couric married Jay Monahan, a lawyer, in 1988. They had two daughters,

Elinor, now 15, and Caroline, now 10. Tragically, Monahan died of colon cancer in 1998, at the age of 42. Couric became an important advocate of cancer detection and a major fundraiser for cancer charities. She considers it the most important work she does.

Couric is happy to sleep in a little later in the morning now. She can spend more time with her daughters. She asked the girls if they thought she

Couric at the Anchor Desk for the CBS Evening News

should take the new job. They encouraged her to go for it. They are a very close family, and Couric's very proud of her girls. "I think they're developing into really fine human beings," she says.

QUOTE

Couric said this about her new job:

"I hope I do this new job with humanity and heart. And intelligence."

Lilly Tartikoff presents Couric with an award for her charity work for cancer research

FOR MORE INFORMATION ABOUT KATIE COURIC:

Write: CBS News
555 West 57th St.
New York, NY 10019

WORLD WIDE WEB SITES:

http://www.cbsnews.com/stories/2006/07/06/evening
news/bios/
http://www.msnbc.msn.com/id/4602812/print/1/
displaymode/1098
http://www.msnbc.msc.com/id/12870221

Vanessa Anne Hudgens
1988-
American Actress and Star of
High School Musical

VANESSA ANNE HUDGENS WAS BORN on December 14, 1988, in Salinas, California. Her parents are Greg and Gina Hudgens. Her dad is part Native American and her mom is Filipino, Chinese, and Spanish. Vanessa has a younger sister named Stella. Stella is also an actress.

VANESSA ANNE HUDGENS GREW UP in San Diego, California. She got the acting bug very young. "I started dancing at 3, acting in community theater at 7, and did my first professional show at 9," she recalls. She got parts in several musicals, including *The Wizard of Oz, The Music Man,* and *Cinderella.*

VANESSA ANNE HUDGENS WENT TO SCHOOL at local schools until seventh grade. Since then, she's been home-schooled.

GETTING INTO SHOW BUSINESS: The family moved to Los Angeles so Vanessa and Stella could continue their acting careers. For Vanessa, that included doing commercials and auditioning for roles.

Soon, Vanessa began to get work in movies. In 2003, she appeared in *Thirteen.* The next year, she landed a role in *Thunderbirds.* She started to get TV roles, too. She appeared in *Quintuplets, The Suite Life of Zack and Cody,* and *Drake & Josh.* But it was her role as Gabriella in the Disney Channel movie *High School Musical* that made her famous.

HIGH SCHOOL MUSICAL: In January 2006, Vanessa appeared in the Disney TV movie *High School Musical.* It was an instant hit, and it made her a star.

Troy (Zac Efron) and Gabriella (Hudgens) meet for the first time, from High School Musical.

The movie is set in a high school in New Mexico. Vanessa plays Gabriella Montez, a brainy, shy girl. On vacation with her family over New Year's, Gabriella gets picked to sing a karaoke song with a boy named Troy. They sing together beautifully. (Troy is played by actor Zac Efron. See the entry on him in the Fall 2006 issue of *Biography for Beginners*.)

Next, the scene shifts back to East High School. Gabriella is just starting at the school. Troy is the star of the basketball team. The two decide to try out for the high school musical. And that's where the problems start.

The main theme of *High School Musical* is being proud of who you are. Gabriella is brainy. The kids on the scholastic decathlon want her on their team. She wants to try something new — singing in the musical. Her new friend Taylor tells her it's not a good idea.

Troy's always been the sports star. Now, he wants to stretch a little, and try out for a musical. His friends on the basketball team tell him he can't.

There's a song and dance scene in the cafeteria that introduces all the groups in the school. There's cheerleaders and athletes, brainy kids and skater kids. They sing about what people think of them, and how that keeps them from being what they truly are.

Then there's Sharpay and Ryan. They're a brother and sister team who've starred in every musical, every year. And they don't want competition.

The stage is set for the first audition. Despite everyone's efforts to keep them apart, Troy and Gabriella perform together. They're called back for a second audition. And, despite Sharpay and Ryan's conniving, Troy and Gabriella triumph. Troy wins the basketball championship, Gabriella wins the science competition, and the two win the starring roles in the musical.

Troy (Efron) and Gabriella (Hudgens) in the finale to
High School Musical.

High School Musical has been a phenomenal success. It's the most-watched movie in the history of the Disney Channel. More than 40 million people have seen it to date. The original soundtrack went to Number 1 on the charts. It was the best- selling CD of 2006. The DVD of the movie, which includes a sing-along version, has sold more than two million copies.

The movie's also produced five hit songs. These include three duets featuring Vanessa and Zac, "Breaking Free," "Start of Something New," and "What I've Been Looking For."

WHAT'S NEXT? Vanessa is a very busy young woman. She's scheduled to appear in *High School Musical 2* in 2007. She's also got a new CD. She's toured the country performing songs from *High School Musical* and her new recording.

QUOTE

"I want to be able to do a wide range of roles. I want to do the Disney movies. I want to do romance. I want to do comedy. So I'm hoping I won't get typecast. But hopefully our acting skills will take us out of that."

VANESSA ANNE HUDGENS'S HOME AND FAMILY:
Vanessa still lives at home with her mom, dad, and sister. She's still trying to get used to her new fame. Recently, she went to the movies with her *High School Musical* co-stars. They were mobbed by fans. "We won't do that again," she said.

SOME OF VANESSA ANNE HUDGENS'S CREDITS:

Thunderbirds
High School Musical

FOR MORE INFORMATION ON VANESSA ANNE HUDGENS:

Write: The Disney Channel
          3800 West Almeda Ave.
          Burbank, CA 91505

WORLD WIDE WEB SITES:

http://psc.disney.go.com/disneychannel/originalmovies/
  highschoolmusical/
http://www.imdb.com/name/nm1374980/

Gordon Parks

1912-2006
American Photographer, Author,
Film Director, and Composer

GORDON PARKS WAS BORN on November 30, 1912, in Fort Scott, Kansas. He was the youngest of 15 children. His parents were Andrew and Sarah Parks. They were farmers. When Gordon was born, his heart wasn't beating.

The doctor plunged him into cold water, and he survived. He was named after the man who saved his life, Dr. Gordon.

GORDON PARKS GREW UP in a poor but loving family. His parents taught him to value equality and the truth. However, the town he lived in was segregated. Gordon grew up at a time when black people did not have the same rights as white people. Blacks could not buy houses or find jobs where they wanted. In most places, they couldn't use the same buildings as white people. Blacks had to use different restaurants, movie theaters, even drinking fountains. They went to segregated schools.

GORDON PARKS WENT TO SCHOOL at the local public schools. His mother died when he was 15. It was a time of great sadness and change. He was sent to live with an older sister and her husband in St. Paul, Minnesota. However, he had a quarrel with his brother-in-law and had to leave the house. He never finished high school. Soon, he was homeless and in need of a job.

EARLY JOBS: Parks's mom had taught him to play piano. In St. Paul, he found work playing in a bar and singing in a band. He also worked as a waiter and mopped floors. When the band left for New York City,

Parks followed them. He lived in the black neighborhood of Harlem and struggled to find work.

In 1933 Parks took a job with the Civilian Conservation Corps. That was a federal program that found work for people on public-service projects. This was during the Depression. It was a time when up to 25% of the population was out of work.

In 1933 Parks married Sally Alvis. He decided to return to St. Paul. In 1934 the couple had a son, Gordon Parks Jr. They would have two more children, a daughter, Toni, and a son, David.

Parks worked at various jobs to support his family. He was a busboy and a waiter, and briefly a semi-pro basketball player. In 1937 he took a job as a waiter on a train. That job would lead to a new career.

While on a trip to Seattle, Parks picked up a magazine left by a passenger. It included a photo essay on migrant workers. (Migrant workers are seasonal workers who move around the country doing farm work and other jobs.) The photographers who took the pictures worked for the Farm Security Administration (FSA). That was a Depression-era agency that hired photographers and writers to show how people were living around the country.

Parks at the office of the Farm Security Administration, 1943

In Seattle, Parks bought his first camera. He took some pictures at the Seattle waterfront. Back home in Minnesota, he dropped the film off at a camera store to be developed. The manager was impressed with his work and displayed the photos.

A CAREER IN PHOTOGRAPHY: Parks began to find work in St. Paul as a fashion photographer. His photos were noticed by Marva Louis. She was the wife of heavyweight boxing champion Joe Louis. Marva encouraged Parks to move to Chicago. He started to work in Chicago's South Side neighborhood. He did fashion photography, and also took photos of life in the city's slums.

Parks's photos won him a Julius Rosenwald Fellowship. It paid him $200 per month. It also allowed him to choose a new career. Parks decided to move to Washington, D.C. He went to work in 1942 for the FSA's photography section. The staff included some of the country's best photographers.

"AMERICAN GOTHIC": On his first day in Washington, Parks took one of his most famous photographs. He called it "American Gothic, Washington, D.C." It shows an African-American cleaning woman, Ella Watson, posed with her broom and mop in front of an American flag.

It seemed like a simple photo. But the story behind it wasn't simple at all. Watson's mother had died and her father had been killed by a lynch mob. Her husband was accidentally shot to death two days before their first child was born.

Parks's choice of the name of his famous photo is important, too. It recalls a famous painting by Grant Wood, "American Gothic." That painting shows an old farm couple, with pitchfork, in front of their barn. Park's

*Photograph of Ella Watson, with her daughter and
three grandchildren, taken by Parks, 1942*

photo shows, with compassion and concern, another
American life, the life of an African-American.

After the FSA closed in 1943, Parks worked briefly
for the Office of War Information. World War II had
begun for the U.S. in 1941. One of his assignments was
to cover the 332nd Fighter Group. That was the first unit
of black fighter pilots in the U.S. Then, someone in the
government decided he couldn't cover the story. Parks
quit his job and moved back to Harlem.

COMMERCIAL SUCCESS: Parks again looked for work in the world of fashion photography. He faced prejudice again, when the magazine *Harper's Bazaar* wouldn't hire him because he was black. But the world-famous photographer Edward Steichen came to his aid. Steichen had seen Parks's work. He recommended him to the editors of *Vogue* and *Glamour* magazines. By the end of 1944 Park's photos had appeared in both publications.

LIFE **MAGAZINE:** In 1948 Parks was hired to work for *Life* magazine. At that time, *Life* was one of the most popular magazines in the country. He was the magazine's first black staff photographer. He continued to work for them until 1972, logging more than 300 assignments.

During that time he covered everything: celebrities, urban crime, poverty, poetry, and the Civil Rights Movement. Sometimes he wrote essays to go along with his photos. Over the years, his subjects included musicians Louis Armstrong and Duke Ellington, writer Langston Hughes, boxer Muhammad Ali, and Black Muslim leader Malcolm X. He also covered the fashion world, and was sent on assignments to Italy, Spain, Portugal, and Brazil.

THE LEARNING TREE: In 1963 Parks wrote an autobiographical novel, *The Learning Tree*. It was based on his early life. *The Learning Tree* was a great success, and was translated into several languages. In 1968, he began a movie career, producing and directing the movie version.

Parks was the first African-American to direct a movie for a major Hollywood studio. He followed *The Learning Tree* with another hit, *Shaft*. That 1971 movie was a huge commercial success.

Parks continued to produce movies and television documentaries. He also continued his writing and photography. He wrote two more autobiographical works and several volumes of poetry, accompanied by photographs. He also co-founded the magazine *Essence*.

Parks made his mark in other artistic fields, too. He composed classical and blues music. In 1989 he wrote the musical score and libretto for a ballet, *Martin*. It was a tribute to the life of Dr. Martin Luther King, Jr. Parks published several collections of his photographs. In 1998 he donated 227 pieces of his work to Washington's Corcoran Gallery of Art. He continued to experiment with new methods in photography, including computerized techniques.

How it feels to be black in the white man's world...

The Learning Tree

A novel from life by Gordon Parks

*Parks Receiving the National Medal of Arts from
President Ronald Reagan, 1988*

Gordon Parks died in his New York City home on
March 7, 2006. He was 93 years old. His funeral was
attended by hundreds of mourners. Many were
photojournalists he had inspired.

From humble beginnings and with little education,
Gordon Parks rose to become one of the most famous
and productive artists of his time. He embodied courage
in the face of prejudice and injustice. He dedicated his
vision and his voice to a wide range of art.

GORDON PARK'S HOME AND FAMILY: Parks was married three times. He and his first wife, Sally, were married in 1933. They had three children, Gordon Jr., Toni, and David. They divorced in 1961. In 1962 Parks married Elizabeth Campbell. The couple had one daughter, Leslie, and were divorced in 1973. In 1973, Parks married his third wife, Genevieve Young. They divorced in 1979.

Parks was honored in his lifetime with 45 honorary degrees. In 1988, President Ronald Reagan awarded him the Medal of Arts. In 2002 he was inducted into the International Photography Hall of Fame. That same year, he received the Jackie Robinson Foundation Lifetime Achievement Award.

QUOTE

"I chose my camera as a weapon against all the things I dislike about America — poverty, racism, discrimination. I could have just as easily picked up a knife or a gun. But I chose not to go that way. I felt that somehow I could subdue these evils by doing something beautiful that people recognize me by."

FOR MORE INFORMATION ABOUT GORDON PARKS:

Write: Gordon Parks Center for Culture & Diversity
Ft. Scott Community College
2108 S. Horton
Fort Scott, KS 66701

WORLD WIDE WEB SITES:

http://www.gordonparkscenter.org/
http://library.pittstate.edu/spcoll/ndxparks.html

Katherine Paterson
1932-
American Writer for Children
and Young Adults
Author of *The Bridge to Terabithia*

KATHERINE PATERSON WAS BORN on October 31, 1932, in Qing Jiang, China. "Paterson" became her last name when she got married. Her name when she was born was Katherine Clements Womeldorf. Her parents were George and Mary Womeldorf. They were

Presbyterian missionaries. Katherine was one of five children. She has one brother, Raymond, and two sisters, Helen and Elizabeth. Another brother, Charles, died as an infant.

KATHERINE PATERSON GREW UP in both China and the United States. She lived in China until she was five years old. In 1938, China and Japan went to war. That forced the family to return to the U.S. They lived in Virginia for a year, then went back to China.

Back in China, her father continued his missionary work. But for their safety, the rest of the family lived in Shanghai. Paterson remembers writing a letter to her father at the time, telling him how much she missed him. When World War II began in 1939, they all returned to the U.S.

KATHERINE PATERSON WENT TO SCHOOL when she returned to America. The family first settled in Winston-Salem, North Carolina, and she started school there. She was painfully shy, and her family moved often. That meant it was hard to make friends, and harder still to leave them.

Paterson often turned to reading for comfort. When she was little, her mother read to her, and she loved the books of A.A. Milne and Beatrix Potter. When she was a little older, her favorite was *The Secret Garden* by Frances

Hodgson Burnett. In fact, she says that "All of my work is an attempt to write something that will touch a reader the way *The Secret Garden* affected me at eight."

Paterson was writing plays for her friends to perform by sixth grade. "I loved those plays," she recalls. "I was a very shy child who loved to show off." She claims that when she was 10, she wanted to be a movie star. But she also thought about following her parents' calling and becoming a missionary.

Paterson was a good student, and she enjoyed acting in school plays. After graduating from high school she went to King College in Tennessee. She loved her English classes, and avoided math "whenever possible."

FIRST JOBS: After graduating from college, Paterson taught sixth grade at a school in rural Virginia. Her students made a vivid impression on her. She says that "almost all my children were like Jesse Aarons." He is the main character in her best-loved novel, *Bridge to Terabithia.*

TRAINING FOR MISSIONARY WORK: Paterson is a devout Christian, and had always wanted to be a missionary. She went back to school, studying Bible and Christian education. She hoped to return to China. But by the time she was ready for mission work, China had closed its borders to most of the outside world.

Paterson went to work in Japan instead. At first, she was frightened. Japan had been America's enemy in World War II. But she fell in love with the people and the country.

BACK TO THE U.S.: Patterson spent four years in Japan. She returned to the U.S. to continue her religious studies. There, she fell in love with John Paterson, who was studying to be a minister. They married in 1962, and soon had four children.

STARTING TO WRITE FOR CHILDREN: It was in the midst of her busy life as a mother that Paterson discovered her true love: writing. "In the cracks of time between feedings, diaperings, cooking, reading aloud, walking to the park, getting still another baby, and carpooling to nursery school, I wrote and wrote."

A friend suggested she take a course in creative writing. That's where she began what would become her first novel. That book, *The Sign of the Chrysanthemum*, is set in Japan. It was the first of three books set in Japan that featured a young person as the main character.

BRIDGE TO TERABITHIA: Paterson's most famous work is *Bridge to Terabithia,* published in 1977. The story was inspired by two life-changing events. At the age of 41, Paterson learned she had cancer. She had surgery and was recovering when tragedy struck. Her son David's best friend, Lisa Hill, was hit by lightning and died. It was a horrible loss. Paterson wrote the book to try to make sense of Lisa's death for David.

The novel tells the story of two friends, Jesse and Leslie, who are outsiders in their rural community. They create a fantasy world, Terabithia. But their imaginary world is shattered when Leslie dies. Paterson shows how Jess begins to face his shattering grief and live again.

Bridge to Terabithia has been a favorite book with young readers for 30 years. It won Paterson the Newbery Medal in 1978. That is the highest honor in children's books.

Bridge to Terabithia was made into a movie in 2007. David Paterson was the producer of the picture. Many young readers think that the movie captured the special magic of Paterson's book.

THE GREAT GILLY HOPKINS: Paterson's next book also reflected a deeply felt family experience. Gilly Hopkins is a foster child who is sassy, funny, and can't get along with her foster mother. Paterson shows how Gilly learns to accept love and family. The author said the book was based on her own experience. "I was once a foster mother and not nearly as good a one as I meant to be," she says.

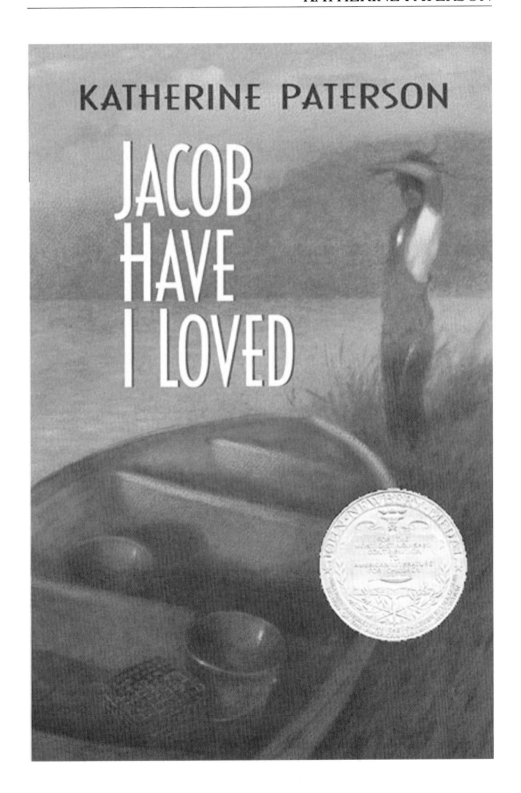

JACOB HAVE I LOVED: In 1980, Paterson published *Jacob Have I Loved*. It is the story of twin girls, Louise and Caroline. The title is taken from the Bible story of Jacob and Esau. "Jacob have I loved, Esau have I hated," reads the passage. In Paterson's book, Louise feels alone and unloved. Her twin sister, the beautiful and talented Caroline, receives all the attention. The book explores jealousy and the meaning of love.

FOR YOUNGER READERS: Paterson has also written picture books for younger readers. One of the best-known is *The King's Equal*. It tells the story of a selfish prince who cannot become king until he finds a woman equal to him in beauty, intelligence, and wealth. Prince Raphael learns the true meaning of those qualities in the story.

ADVICE TO YOUNG WRITERS: Paterson is often asked for advice from young people who want to write. She believes that would-be writers need to get up the courage and just write. "There are no guarantees. It takes courage to lay your insides out for people to examine and sneer over. But that's the only way to give what is your unique gift to the world. I have often noted that it takes the thinnest skin in the world to be a writer. It takes the thickest to seek out publication. But both are needed — the extreme sensitivity and the hippo hide against criticism. Send your inner critic off on vacation and just write the way little children play."

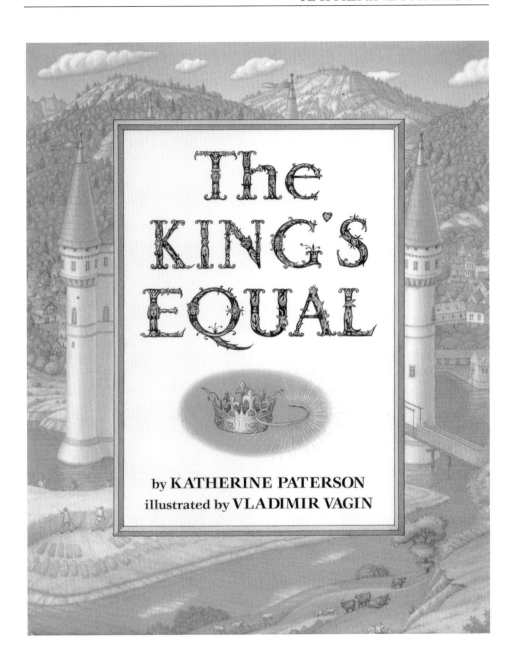

KATHERINE PATERSON'S HOME AND FAMILY:

Paterson has been married for 45 years to John Paterson. She says he is the greatest influence on her work, and her greatest champion.

They have two sons, John Jr. and David. They also have two adopted daughters. Elizabeth PoLin came to the Patersons from China. (PoLin means "precious life" in Chinese). Mary Katherine Nah-he-sah-pe-che-a is from an Apache reservation. Her last name means "young Apache lady."

Paterson enjoys spending time with her family, especially her many grandchildren. She also still loves to read, and enjoys playing piano and tennis. She and her husband live in Vermont.

QUOTE

Paterson wrote this about the struggle of bringing characters and a story to life.

"Eventually a character or characters will walk into my imagination and begin to take over my life. I'll spend the next couple of years getting to know them and telling their story. Then the joy of writing far outweighs the struggle, and I know beyond any doubt that I am the most fortunate person in the world to have been given such work to do."

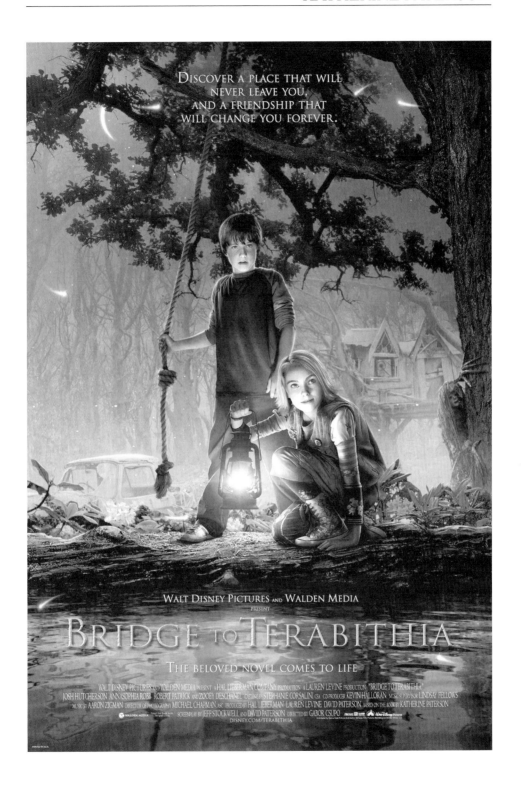

SOME OF KATHERINE PATERSON'S BOOKS:

For Middle Grade Readers:
The Sign of the Chrysanthemum
The Master Puppeteer
Bridge to Terabithia
The Great Gilly Hopkins
Jacob Have I Loved
Come Sing, Jimmy Jo
Lyddie
Jip, His Story
Preacher's Boy

For Early Readers:
Angels and Other Strangers
The Tale of the Mandarin Ducks
The King's Equal
The Flip-Flop Girl
The Angel and the Donkey
Marvin's Best Christmas Present Ever
Celia and the Sweet, Sweet Water

FOR MORE INFORMATION:

Write: Clarion Books
215 Park Ave. South
New York, NY 1003

WORLD WIDE WEB SITES:

http://www.falcon.jmu.edu/~ramseyil/paterson.htm
http://www.ipl.org/div/kispace/askauthor/paterson.html
http://www.terabithia.com

David Wiesner

1956-
American Children's Author and Illustrator
Three-Time Caldecott Medal Winner
Creator of *Tuesday, The Three Pigs,*
and *Flotsam*

DAVID WIESNER WAS BORN on February 5, 1956, in Bridgewater, New Jersey. His parents are George and Julia Wiesner. George was a chemist and Julia was a homemaker. He has a sister named Carol and a brother named George.

DAVID WIESNER GREW UP in a family that encouraged his imagination. He loved to play with friends in the woods near his home. They'd play "war" for hours. They'd pretend to be among dinosaurs, or on another planet.

David also loved to watch his sister and brother paint and draw. He also loved a TV show that taught viewers how to draw. Soon, he was asking for paint sets. He'd draw and paint, letting his imagination run wild.

At night, before sleep, David would stare into the darkness. Images from his bedroom wallpaper — rockets, elephants, clocks — would feed his imagination as he drifted off.

Another source of inspiration was cartoons. Wiesner remembers a particular Bugs Bunny episode. Bugs and Elmer Fudd run off the screen, "right off the frame of the film." "To me, at seven or eight, it was more than funny. When I saw this cartoon, I laughed, and at the same time gasped. The idea of the characters running out of one reality into another left me astounded."

THE LIBRARY: David was inspired by books, too. He pored over the encyclopedia at home, thrilling to the animal pictures. He also made many trips to the library.

"The library opened my eyes to other ways of seeing. It was in the stacks of the Bound Brook, New Jersey, public library that I pored over the Time/Life series of books about the great artists." He especially liked the works of Leonardo Da Vinci. "I particularly loved the background landscapes," he recalls. "Have you ever looked really closely at the scene behind the "Mona Lisa"? There's no place like that on earth. It could be Mars."

Wiesner also loved the Surrealists. That group of artists created paintings full of bizarre images. They made a great impression on him and his art.

DAVID WIESNER WENT TO SCHOOL: At the local public schools in New Jersey. He did well in school, and loved art class. He went to high school at Bridgewater Raritan East. There, his art teacher became a great influence.

Wiesner developed a love for science fiction and fantasy. He loved horror movies, and the near-silent movie *2001: A Space Odyssey.* He was captivated by wordless storytelling. He wanted to draw pictures that expressed a story without words.

Many readers think Wiesner's books look like movies. That makes sense, because he loves to think about what happens "around" a picture. What comes before, and what comes after, an individual picture fascinates him. He even made a movie in high school, *The Saga of Butchala*, about a vampire.

He showed *Butchala* in the senior talent show. It was a great hit. He calls it "one of the high points of high school. The audience reacted at all the right points. I experienced this incredible feeling. It was great!"

Wiesner went to the Rhode Island School of Design (RISD) for college. That's one of the finest art schools in the country. One of his teachers was David Macaulay, a well-known children's author and illustrator. Macaulay and his other teachers taught Wiesner how to paint and draw. But they also helped him to "see." He learned how to develop his own vision of what a book can be.

STARTING TO CREATE BOOKS FOR CHILDREN: At RISD, Wiesner met Trina Schart Hyman. She was the editor of *Cricket* magazine. She loved Wiesner's work and offered him the opportunity to do a *Cricket* cover. That's how he got started in children's books.

Wiesner moved to New York City and started illustrating books by other authors. In 1980, he illustrated *Honest Andrew* by Gloria Skurzynski. That same year, he drew the pictures for Avi's *Man from the Sky*.

Wiesner still dreamed of writing and illustrating his own work. He began working on several ideas. But all that ended when his apartment burned down. He started over.

In 1987, Wiesner produced his first book as author and illustrator, *The Loathsome Dragon*. It was the first in a series of some of the finest and most popular books for children.

TUESDAY: One of his readers' favorites is *Tuesday*. It features frogs — everywhere. They watch TV, chase dogs, and fly through the air. *Tuesday* was a great success with readers young and old. It won Wiesner the Caldecott Medal. That's the highest honor in children's book illustration.

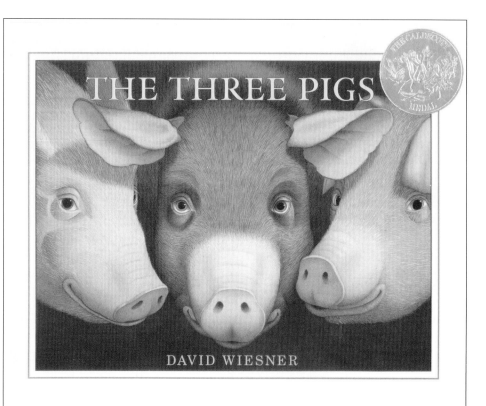

THE THREE PIGS: Another favorite with young readers
is *The Three Pigs*. Wiesner takes the old story and
stands it on its head. He explores one of his favorite
ideas — what happens *outside* the pictures of a story. In
his version, the wolf blows the first and second pigs
"right out of the story." So they're not there to be eaten
up. The poor wolf!

The pigs have a delightful time, exploring the world
outside the story that had held them "captive." Their
journey ends at home, but with a funny twist, with

characters from other children's stories. This lively and inventive book captivated readers everywhere. It won Wiesner his second Caldecott Medal.

FLOTSAM: Wiesner's most recent book is *Flotsam.* This wordless book begins on the seashore. A young boy discovers a mysterious camera floating in the ocean. He develops the photos, which take him on a fantastic journey of discovery. Children, sea creatures, and wondrous images float across the pages of this astonishing book.

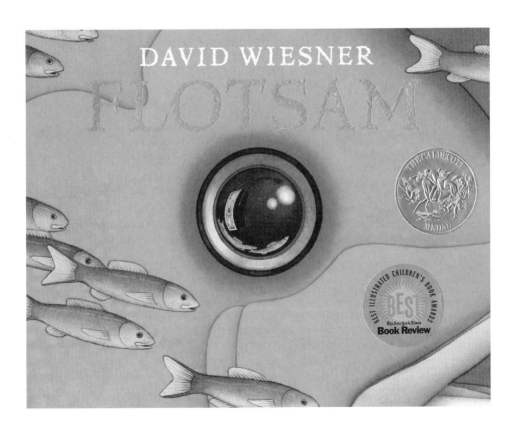

For *Flotsam*, Wiesner won his third Caldecott Medal. He is only the second person to win the honor three times. Two of his other books, *Sector 7* and *Free Fall*, received the Caldecott Honor award. Wiesner has also received book prizes from other countries. This honored author continues to create books that delight and challenge readers everywhere.

DAVID WIESNER'S HOME AND FAMILY: Wiesner is married to Kim Kahng. She is a surgeon and has also worked on books with David. They have a son, Kevin, and daughter, Jaime. They live in Philadelphia.

QUOTE

"It's a wonderful thing, the picture book. It's this set size and shape that you have to work with. There's a title page and there's a page where the copyright material goes. But what's really fun is to be able to see what you can do within the confines of that format, see how far you can push it and whether there's something new you can do with it. I enjoy the challenge of it."

SOME OF DAVID WIESNER'S BOOKS:

As Author and Illustrator:

The Loathsome Dragon

Free Fall

Hurricane

Tuesday

June 29, 1999

Sector 7

The Three Pigs

Flotsam

As Illustrator:

Honest Andrew

Man from the Sky

The Boy Who Spoke Chimp

Neptune Rising

Firebrat

The Rainbow People

Tongues of Jade

Night of the Gargoyles

FOR MORE INFORMATION ABOUT DAVID WIESNER:

Write: Clarion Books
215 Park Avenue South
New York, NY 10003

WORLD WIDE WEB SITES:

http://www.bookpage.com/9909bp/david_wiesner.html

http://www.clarionbooks.com

http://www.houghtonmifflinbooks.com/authors/wiesner
  /bio/

http:/www.loc.gov/today/cyberlc/feature_wdesc.

http://www.rif.org/art/illustrators/wiesner.mspx

Mo Willems

1968-
American Author, Illustrator, and Animator
Creator of *Don't Let the Pigeon Drive the Bus!* and *Knuffle Bunny*

MO WILLEMS WAS BORN in 1968 in New Orleans. He doesn't reveal a lot of information about his personal life. His parents are immigrants, and his father is a potter. Mo is an only child.

MO WILLEMS GREW UP loving to tell jokes and draw. He loved to read comics, especially "Peanuts." "I loved to draw Charlie Brown and Snoopy," he recalls. "By second or third grade, I made comics out of my own character: Laser Brain! He was a space hero who'd lost his brain in a horrible laser accident."

MO WILLEMS WENT TO SCHOOL at the local public schools. He has a bad memory of art class. His art teacher told him to stop drawing cartoons. "She said big, boring drawings of fruit in a bowl were A-R-T. But funny cartoons that made people laugh weren't. She was wrong."

By high school, Mo was doing stand-up comedy in local clubs. He says he wasn't very funny, but he kept at it. He also acted in plays and made films with his friends. Instead of heading to college after high school, Mo went to England. He spent a year doing stand-up in London comedy clubs.

Willems returned to America and started college at New York University. He majored in film studies. Soon, he was captivated by the world of animation. Willems says he loved animation for two reasons. One, it was cheap. He didn't have to pay for actors and props. And, in animation, the artist is in complete control.

Willems began making animated films and studying them, too. He was especially influenced by old cartoonists. The last film he made in school was "The Man Who Yelled." Willems says he used it as his "calling card" to find jobs.

From Sheep in the Big City

SESAME STREET: Willems wound up, through "luck and hard work," working on *Sesame Street*. He started out drawing smiley faces for the research department. Then he was invited to audition. They loved his work, and he wrote for the series from 1994 to 2002.

Willems loved working on *Sesame Street.* He says it taught him a lot. "On *Sesame Street* you have to teach a particular concept in a particular way." It also must be "entertaining and original." "Every word has to count," he says, so he learned to cut down his language.

He also learned another thing that's stayed with him all his career. "Funny is funny," he says. "And that's true whether you're writing for kids or adults." Willems won six Emmys for his work on *Sesame Street.* One of his creations was "Elmo's World." That feature starred Elmo, who was created by Kevin Clash. (See the profile of Clash in this issue of *Biography for Beginners.)*

SHEEP IN THE BIG CITY and **CODENAME: KIDS NEXT DOOR:** While working at *Sesame Street*, Willems started to create his own cartoon series. *Sheep in the Big City* featured a poor sheep on the run from bad guys. It ran on the Cartoon Network for several years. Willems next worked on *Codename: Kids Next Door.* He was head writer of the show for several years.

STARTING TO WRITE FOR KIDS: After eight years in TV, Mo was ready for something else. "When I had my television show, I worked like mad, writing, directing, doing voices, designing characters, doing *Sesame Street*. When it was over, I realized that I'd forgotten to have any *fun.*"

He decided to try something else. He spent some time in England, living in a cottage. He tried writing books, but nothing worked out. Finally, an idea came to him for a story based on a pigeon. He created a sketch-book of ideas. An agent saw the book and loved it. The rest, as they say, is history.

DON'T LET THE PIGEON DRIVE THE BUS! Willems's first book features a wily pigeon who can't wait to take over the bus when the driver goes on break. Even though the driver has *asked* the reader to keep the pigeon out of the driver's seat, the bird has other ideas.

Young readers love Willems's very silly book. And they couldn't wait for more. The book won him his first Caldecott Honor. That's one of the highest honors in children's book illustration. The Pigeon returns in such favorites as *The Pigeon Finds a Hot Dog!* and *Don't Let the Pigeon Stay Up Late!*

KNUFFLE BUNNY: Another favorite Willems book is based on his experiences with his daughter, Trixie. It features a dad and daughter on a trip to the laundromat. On the way home, Trixie realizes her beloved bunny is missing. She can't talk yet, but she's so unhappy, her dad knows something's horribly wrong. Mom saves the day, and the book has a happy — and hilarious — ending.

Willems adapted the story for an animated film. The *Knuffle Bunny* movie was a great success. It also won Willems a Carnegie Medal, a high honor in film.

EDWINA, THE DINOSAUR WHO DIDN'T KNOW SHE WAS EXTINCT: One of Willems's recent books features a delightful dinosaur named Edwina. Everyone loves Edwina. They love her chocolate chip cookies, too. But the know-it-all Reginald Von Hoobie-Doobie sets out to prove Edwina is Extinct. The results are warm, and really funny, too.

THE FUTURE: Willems says he's an incredibly lucky guy. He's not sure what the future will bring, but insists it's going to be fun. "Picture books are a second chance for me. So, while I occasionally yearn to spend my life squirreled away in my studio, drawing while ignoring the travel, speeches, and business, I know that's impractical. I simply have to have as much fun as possible no matter what I'm doing."

MO WILLEMS'S HOME AND FAMILY: Willems lives with his wife, Cheryl, and daughter, Trixie, in Brooklyn, New York. He says his wife is "funnier, more insightful, and looks better in heels than I do."

Mo works out of his home, in a studio. He loves being home with Trixie, and eating lunch with his family every day. When an idea hits him, he "squishes it into one of my notebooks." Then, "the trick of keeping it alive and nursing it to strength takes place in my Brooklyn studio."

QUOTE

Mo Willems has this to say about writing books for kids:

"I write silly books for *people*. It just happens to be that usually kids are the first people silly enough to enjoy them."

"I can only hope that whatever's next will stick to my guiding principle: Always think *of* your audience, never think *for* your audience."

SOME OF MO WILLEMS CREDITS:

Television and Film

Sesame Street, 1994-2002
The Off-Beats, 1995-1998
Sheep in the Big City, 2000-2002
Codename: The Kids Next Door, 2001-2002
Knuffle Bunny

Books

Don't Let the Pigeon Drive the Bus!
Knuffle Bunny: A Cautionary Tale
Pigeon Finds a Hot Dog!

The Pigeon Has Feelings, Too!
Don't Let the Pigeon Stay Up Late!
The Pigeon Loves Things That Go!
Edwina, the Dinosaur Who Didn't Know She Was Extinct
Time to Pee!
Time to Say 'Please'!
You Can Never Find a Rickshaw When it Monsoons: The World on One Cartoon a Day
Leonardo, The Terrible Monster
Knuffle Bunny Too: A Case of Mistaken Identity
My Friend is Sad! An Elephant and Piggie Early Reader
Today I Will Fly! An Elephant and Piggie Early Reader

FOR MORE INFORMATION ABOUT MO WILLEMS:

Write: Hyperion Books for Children
114 5th Ave.
14th Floor
New York, NY 10011

WORLD WIDE WEB SITES:

http://www.bookpage.com/0307bp/meet_mo_willem.html
http://www.mowillems.com
http://hyperionbooksforchildren.com
http://powells.com/kidsqa/willems.html
http://www.theedgeoftheforest.com

Name Index

Listed below are the names of all individuals who have appeared in *Biography for Beginners,* followed by the issue and year in which they appear.

Subject Index

This index includes subjects, occupations, and ethnic and minority origins for individuals who have appeared in *Biography for Beginners.*

Sachar, Louis, Spring 2002
Scarry, Richard, Spring '95
Scieszka, Jon, Fall '95
Sendak, Maurice, Spring '96
Seuss, Dr., Spring '95
Shannon, David, Fall 2006
Silverstein, Shel, Spring '97
Sis, Peter, Fall 2004
Small, David, Fall 2002
Steig, William, Spring 2000
Van Allsburg, Chris,
  Spring '96
Viorst, Judith, Fall 2006
Wells, Rosemary, Spring '96
White, E.B., Spring 2002
Wiesner, David,
  Spring 2007
Wilder, Laura Ingalls,
  Fall '96
Willard, Nancy, Spring
  2004
Williams, Garth, Fall '96
Willems, Mo , Spring 2007
Wood, Audrey, Spring 2003
Wood, Don, Spring 2003
Yolen, Jane, Spring '99

autobiographer
Angelou, Maya, Fall 2006

baseball players
Bonds, Barry, Fall 2002

Griffey, Ken Jr., Fall '95
Jeter, Derek, Fall 2000
Martinez, Pedro,
  Spring 2001
McGwire, Mark, Spring '99
Ripken, Cal Jr., Fall '96
Sosa, Sammy, Spring '99
Suzuki, Ichiro, Fall 2003

basketball players
Bryant, Kobe, Fall '99
Carter, Vince, Fall 2001
Duncan, Tim, Fall 2005
Hill, Grant, Fall '97
Jordan, Michael, Spring '97
Leslie, Lisa, Fall 2006
Olajuwon, Hakeem,
  Spring '96
O'Neal, Shaquille, Fall '95
Robinson, David, Fall '96
Swoopes, Sheryl,
  Spring 2000

bicycle racer
Armstrong, Lance, Fall 2002

black
Adu, Freddy, Spring 2005
Angelou, Maya, Fall 2006
Annan, Kofi, Fall 2000
Barber, Ronde, Spring 2004
Barber, Tiki, Spring 2004

illustrators

Birthday Index

January

7 Katie Couric (1957)
12 John Lasseter (1957)
14 Shannon Lucid (1943)
17 Shari Lewis (1934)
21 Hakeem Olajuwon (1963)
26 Vince Carter (1977)
28 Wayne Gretzky (1961)
29 Bill Peet (1915)
Rosemary Wells (1943)
Oprah Winfrey (1954)
30 Dick Cheney (1941)
31 Bryan Collier (1967)

February

2 Judith Viorst (1931)
4 Rosa Parks (1913)
5 David Wiesner (1956)
7 Laura Ingalls Wilder (1867)
9 Wilson "Snowflake" Bentley (1865)
11 Jane Yolen (1939)
Brandy (1979)
12 Judy Blume (1938)
David Small (1945)
13 Mary GrandPré (1954)
15 Norman Bridwell (1928)
Amy Van Dyken (1973)

February (continued)

16 LeVar Burton (1957)
17 Michael Jordan (1963)
22 Steve Irwin (1962)
24 Steven Jobs (1955)
27 Chelsea Clinton (1980)

March

2 Dr. Seuss (1904)
David Satcher (1941)
3 Patricia MacLachlan (1938)
Jackie Joyner-Kersee (1962)
4 Garrett Morgan (1877)
Dav Pilkey (1966)
5 Mem Fox (1946)
Jake Lloyd (1989)
6 Chris Raschka (1959)
8 Robert Sabuda (1965)
10 Shannon Miller (1977)
11 Ezra Jack Keats (1916)
12 Virginia Hamilton (1936)
15 Ruth Bader Ginsburg (1933)
16 Shaquille O'Neal (1972)
17 Mia Hamm (1972)
18 Bonnie Blair (1964)

March (continued)

20 Fred Rogers (1928)
 Lois Lowry (1937)
 Louis Sachar (1954)
21 Rosie O'Donnell (1962)
25 DiCamillo, Kate (1964)
 Sheryl Swoopes (1971)
 Danica Patrick (1982)
31 Al Gore (1948)

April

3 Jane Goodall (1934)
 Amanda Bynes (1986)
4 Maya Angelou (1928)
5 Colin Powell (1937)
 Dean Kamen (1951)
7 RondeBarber (1975)
 Tiki Barber (1975)
8 Kofi Annan (1938)
12 Beverly Cleary (1916)
 Tony Hawk (1968)
15 Tim Duncan (1976)
 Emma Watson (1990)
16 Garth Williams (1912)
18 Melissa Joan Hart
 (1976)
26 Patricia Reilly Giff
 (1935)
27 Ludwig Bemelmans
 (1898)
 Coretta Scott King
 (1927)
 Barbara Park (1947)

May

4 Don Wood (1945)
6 Judy Delton (1931)
 Ted Lewin (1935)
10 Leo Lionni (1910)
 Christopher Paul
 Curtis (1953)
 Ellen Ochoa (1958)
11 Peter Sis (1949)
12 Betsy Lewin (1937)
14 George Lucas (1944)
 Emmitt Smith (1969)
16 Margret Rey (1906)
17 Gary Paulsen (1939)
20 Mary Pope Osborne
 (1949)
22 Arnold Lobel (1933)
23 Margaret Wise Brown
 (1910)
29 Andrew Clements
 (1949)

June

2 Freddy Adu (1989)
5 Richard Scarry (1919)
6 Cynthia Rylant (1954)
7 Larisa Oleynik (1981)
9 Freddie Highmore
 (1992)
10 Maurice Sendak (1928)
 Tara Lipinski (1982)
11 Joe Montana (1956)

June (continued)
13 Tim Allen (1953)
15 Jack Horner (1946)
18 Chris Van Allsburg (1949)
25 Eric Carle (1929)
26 Nancy Willard (1936)
Derek Jeter (1974)
Michael Vick (1980)
30 Robert Ballard (1971)
Michael Phelps (1985)

July
2 Dave Thomas (1932)
6 George W. Bush (1946)
7 Lisa Leslie (1972)
Michelle Kwan (1980)
11 E.B. White (1899)
Patricia Polacco (1944)
12 Kristi Yamaguchi (1972)
13 Stephanie Kwolek (1923)
14 Peggy Parish (1927)
Laura Numeroff (1953)
18 Nelson Mandela (1918)
24 Barry Bonds (1964)
Mara Wilson (1987)
26 Jan Berenstain (1923)
28 Beatrix Potter (1866)
Natalie Babbitt (1932)
Jim Davis (1945)

July (continued)
31 J.K. Rowling (1965)
Daniel Radcliffe (1989)

August
2 Betsy Byars (1928)
3 Tom Brady (1977)
4 Jeff Gordon (1971)
6 Barbara Cooney (1917)
David Robinson (1965)
9 Patricia McKissack (1944)
Whitney Houston (1963)
11 Joanna Cole (1944)
12 Walter Dean Myers (1937)
Fredrick McKissack (1939)
Ann M. Martin (1955)
15 Linda Ellerbee (1944)
16 Matt Christopher (1917)
18 Paula Danziger (1944)
19 Bill Clinton (1946)
21 Stephen Hillenburg (1961)
23 Kobe Bryant (1978)
24 Cal Ripken Jr. (1960)
26 Mother Teresa (1910)
27 Alexandra Nechita (1985)

August (continued)
- **28** Brian Pinkney (1961)
- **29** Temple Grandin (1947)
- **30** Virginia Lee Burton (1909)
  Sylvia Earle (1935)
  Donald Crews (1938)
- **31** Itzhak Perlman (1945)

September
- **1** Gloria Estefan (1958)
- **3** Aliki (1929)
- **7** Briana Scurry (1971)
- **8** Jack Prelutsky (1940)
  Jon Scieszka (1954)
  Jonathan Taylor Thomas (1982)
- **15** McCloskey, Robert (1914)
  Tomie dePaola (1934)
- **16** H. A. Rey (1898)
  Roald Dahl (1916)
- **17** Kevin Clash (1960)
- **18** Ben Carson (1951)
  Lance Armstrong (1971)
- **24** Jim Henson (1936)
- **25** Andrea Davis Pinkney (1963)
- **25** Will Smith (1968)
- **26** Serena Williams (1981)

September (continued)
- **28** Hilary Duff (1987)
- **29** Stan Berenstain (1923)
- **30** Dominique Moceanu (1981)

October
- **1** Mark McGwire (1963)
- **5** Grant Hill (1972)
  Maya Lin (1959)
- **6** Lonnie Johnson (1949)
- **7** Yo-Yo Ma (1955)
- **8** Faith Ringgold (1930)
- **9** Zachery Ty Bryan (1981)
- **10** James Marshall (1942)
- **11** Michelle Wie (1989)
- **12** Marion Jones (1975)
- **13** Nancy Kerrigan (1969)
- **17** Mae Jemison (1954)
  Nick Cannon (1980)
- **18** Wynton Marsalis (1961)
  Zac Efron (1987)
- **22** Ichiro Suzuki (1973)
- **23** Pele (1940)
- **25** Pedro Martinez (1971)
- **26** Hillary Clinton (1947)
  Steven Kellogg (1941)
  Eric Rohmann (1957)
- **28** Bill Gates (1955)
- **31** Katherine Paterson (1932)

November

3 Janell Cannon (1957)
4 Laura Bush (1946)
9 Lois Ehlert (1934)
12 Sammy Sosa (1968)
14 Astrid Lindgren (1907)
William Steig (1907)
Condoleezza Rice
(1954)
15 Daniel Pinkwater
(1941)
19 Savion Glover (1973)
Kerri Strug (1977)
21 Ken Griffey Jr. (1969)
25 Marc Brown (1946)
26 Charles Schulz (1922)
27 Bill Nye (1955)
Kevin Henkes (1960)
Jaleel White (1977)
30 Gordon Parks (1912)

December

1 Jan Brett (1949)
5 Frankie Muniz (1985)
9 Jean de Brunhoff
(1899)
10 Raven (1985)
18 Christina Aguilera
(1980)
14 Vanessa Anne
Hudgens (1988)
19 Eve Bunting (1928)

December (continued)

22 Jerry Pinkney (1939)
23 Avi (1937)
26 Susan Butcher (1954)
30 Mercer Mayer (1943)
Tiger Woods (1975)

Photo and Illustrations Credits

Jean de Brunhoff/Photos: Random House. Covers: THE STORY OF BABAR copyright © 1933, renewed 1961 by Random House, Inc.; THE TRAVELS OF BABAR copyright © 1934, renewed 1962 by Random House, Inc.; BABAR AND FATHER CHRISTMAS copyright © 1940, renewed 1968 by Random House, Inc., and Cecil de Brunhoff.

Kevin Clash/Photos: Deborah Finegold. PR Newswire, PRN/news.com MY LIFE AS A FURRY RED MONSTER courtesy Broadway Books/Random House, Inc. Front cover photo: Nate Lankford, Sesame Street Workshop.

Katie Couric/Photos: CBS Photo/John Paul Filo/CBS copyright © 2006 CBS Broadcasting, Inc. All rights reserved. Courtesy NBC News/Today. PR Newswire, PRN/news.com

Vanessa Anne Hudgens/Photos: AP Images; Disney Channel/Fred Hayes.

Gordon Parks/Photos: Courtesy Ronald Reagan Library; Courtesy Library of Congress. Cover: THE LEARNING TREE copyright © 1963 by Gordon Parks.

Katherine Paterson/Photo: Courtesy of HarperCollins. Covers: THE BRIDGE TO TERABITHIA copyright © 1977 by Katherine Paterson. JACOB HAVE I LOVED copyright © 1980 by Katherine Paterson. THE KING'S EQUAL copyright © 1992 by Katherine Paterson. Movie poster courtesy Buena Vista Pictures.

David Wiesner/Photo: Courtesy Houghton Mifflin Company. Covers: TUESDAY copyright © 1997 by David Wiesner. THE THREE PIGS copyright © 2001 by David Wiesner. FLOTSAM copyright © 2006 by David Wiesner.

Mo Willems/Photo: Courtesy Hyperion Books for Children. SHEEP IN THE BIG CITY: Courtesy Cartoon Network Covers: DON'T LET THE PIGEON DRIVE THE BUS! Copyright © 2003 by Mo Willems. KNUFFLE BUNNY copyright © 2004 by Mo Willems. EDWINA THE DINOSAUR WHO DIDN'T KNOW SHE WAS EXTINCT copyright © 2006 by Mo Willems.